5 Ways A Book Can Help You Grow Your Business

#1 Best Selling Author
Kelly Cole

Look At A Book As Your New Business Card!

Publishing A Book Could Help You:

- Brand Yourself As An Expert
- Create A New Income Stream
- Generate Leads For Your Business
- Elevate Your Platform
- Get More Clients
- Establish Credibility

AUTHORity!!!

"The World's Best Marketing Tool:
Writing a Book"

~ Entrepreneur Magazine

Here's What A Book Will Do For You

- Help You Create Unshakeable Credibility

- It Will Finally Deliver Your Message Into The Hands Of The World

- Set You Apart From Other "Experts" By Placing You Among The Few That Are Best Selling Authors

- Position You To Make More Money Because Of Your Credentials

- Allow You To Leave A Legacy Long After You're Gone

- Open The Door To The Privilege Opportunities That ONLY Published Authors Enjoy

Yes you really can become a bestselling author, Publishing Advantage Group can make that happen for you even if you don't like writing!

We are so good; we can get your book done without you writing a single word!

I know you are saying to yourself how can you do that?

Well it's simple...

All we have to do is get you on the phone, interview you and have our Team of writers turn it into the book!

Everybody has a book in them!

Your book will be filled with your specialized knowledge about your topic or field.

We will help you share yours in a high quality book just like the one you are reading now!

Imagine what your friends and family is going to think when they see it, and you let them hold your book in their hand.

They are going to be so proud of you!

You will be the talk of the town, everybody's perception of you is guaranteed to change, you will not only be now known as an Entrepreneur, you will be a Best Selling Author!

If you've ever **dreamed** of Taking Your Career or Business to the NEXT LEVEL, now is the time!

Today is the day for **YOU** to MAKE IT HAPPEN!

Get started now!

I like you may have gotten started on a book but life happens. A life event happens, your family gets a new baby, you get married, you get a promotion...the manuscript goes in the drawer along with your dream of becoming an author. Instead of sticking with it, starting back when you can, you lose focus and bury your dreams in a drawer along with the hope of ever getting it done.

Stop wasting months and even years procrastinating and get your book done now!

I remember kicking myself mentally because I knew I should write a book and all the benefits awaiting me after I completed.

How does the publishing process work?

There are 3 ways to go about this.

1. If you like to write or already have your book written, You are ahead of the game simply email or call us to find out what the publishing special is for this month. Take action and we could have your book published and on the market in 2 weeks or less!

2. If you don't like to write we can interview you and have one of writers, turn the interview into the book. simply email or call us to find out what the publishing special is for this month and Take Action!

3. You can give us the topic and we can ghostwrite the complete for you!

**Get Started Now Visit:
www.PublishAdvantageGroup.com
or call 276-229-0530**

What are the benefits of becoming a Best Selling Author?

-Brands you as an Instant expert in your field

-Separates You From The Pack!

-Creates several new income streams

-Builds a platform to get PAID Speaking engagements

-Gives a product to sell at appearance / speaking engagements

-Can be used as a lead generator for your business

-Open the doors to countless opportunities that wouldn't be available if you did have a book

Becoming A Best Selling Author will help you Generate Leads, Close More Deals, Establish Credibility!

Who are we and why should you listen to us?

We Are Publish Advantage Group!

We are an book publishing company powered by Prime Time Marketing, we help Entrepreneurs, Speakers, Chiropractors and Realtors become best-selling authors and show them how to use a book as a marketing tool. We help you establish a platform that delivers you with credibility, authority and publicity, which boosts your sales, profits and your unique selling proposition.

We've produced countless best-selling authors in the last 10 years who have been have appeared on OWN, Real House Wives of ATL, Bravo, NBA, WORD network, MTV, BET, Atlantic Records, Capitol Records and more. We provide full publishing & ghostwriting services that will help new and experienced authors boost their income.

About our CEO Kelly Cole

Kelly Cole is a #1 Best Selling Author, Master Book Publishing Strategist & Minister. Kelly has authored and published over 50+ paperback, audio and e-books to date.

Kelly has been seen on NBC, FOX, ABC, The CW, Gospel Updates Magazine & more. Kelly started Prime Time Marketing 12 Years ago after quitting his day job at Wal-Mart, He almost ended up homeless but worked hard serving and helping other people dreams come true, which ultimately led to his dream coming true of building a successful marketing & publishing company. In 2014 he was even elected into the GrindMoves Hall of Fame.

He has been labeled A Business Guru for his knowledge and marketing wisdom that he has used to help people all over the world!

He is the proud father of three, 1 Boy & 2 Girls and married for over 15 years to Natasha.

When You Publish With Us, You keep 100% of your rights and 100% of your profits!

You retain 100% of the rights and copyright licenses to your manuscript and all other materials submitted to Publishing Advantage Group.

Your book will be available for order through online retail sales channels like Amazon, Barnes & Noble, Books-A-Million, and more. Plus, with our amazing *distribution-on-demand* your book can be available for order from just about anywhere that sells books.

One of the best features of our publishing package our print on-demand service! Every time an order comes in you don't have to touch a thing. The system will print and ship your book directly to your customer.

Plus You Get Complete print-run flexibility, meaning you don't have to order a bunch of books to get started with us. And whenever you decide you want book there is no minimum you have to order, you can order 1 to 1000s! It's totally up to you!

You never have to order any books unless you want to. Of course, if you want to order books, you always receive a wholesale price.

If you've always dreamed of Taking Your Career or Business to the NEXT LEVEL, Today Is The Day!

Once you have your book published ... it's evergreen! That means, long after you've gone on to new things, you can still reap the benefits and best of all **passive income** that keeps coming!

Creating an book using your information is one of the fastest and most profitable ways to make more money.

You don't have to worry anymore about whether your message is significant - Thousands will pay for your unique knowledge.

You become the expert in your field - A book will create instant credibility and trust with your clients.

Just think, you don't have to sit on the side lines anymore watching the parade of best-selling authors go by.

You can lead the parade with your own best-selling book spreading over the internet like wild fire.

It will be one of the smallest investments made into your marketing to reap such HUGE benefits and profits.

Wouldn't it be wonderful to:

- Impress Your Friends And Family When You Tell Them To Lookup & Order Your New Book On Amazon.com!

- Pull In More Business By Handing Your Prospects You're a Copy Of Your Book And Telling Them Its Availability On Amazon.com!

Create A New Income Stream For Your Business Or To Supplement Your Current Income! Mannn the feeling of actually becoming a best-selling author, I just can't describe it. But, you'll find out yourself !

Check out some of the Authors we've published!

This young lady is Jessie Rogers, **she is 16 and was born blind.** We made her dream of becoming a published author come True!

WOW She is 16 & Born Blind and you're still making excuses?

Keith "Mister" Jennings is an American basketball Coach, Author, Speaker & Trainer who formerly played in the NBA for The Golden State Warriors & Denver Nuggets.

Tawana R. Powell
Best Selling Author, Speaker, Journalist & Inspirational Enlightenment Coach

Chandler Coleman
Best Selling Author,
Entrepreneur, Pastor &
Fitness Coach

Terence-Humphrey Gbassagee
Best Selling Author,
Entrepreneur, Pastor &
Apostle

"Prime Time Marketing did a Wonderful Job Publishing my book!

People need whats in your hands, get with Prime Time Marketing you will be so Happy you did!

Dr. Stewart McClain
Author of "Living In The Overflow"

I Would Not Have Been Able To This Without Kelly and His Team!

I'm selling books like CRAZY!

If you ever need your book done Kelly is The Man To Go To!

Paul Crick
Author of "Cricks Relationship Langauge"

With writing my first book, Kelly Cole & Prime Time Marketing have exceeded my expectations.

Kelly's love for what he does pleasantly flowed into every aspect of the publishing process.

His drive and ability to go beyond expectations enforces my desire to work with him and Prime Time Marketing again soon.

Tawana R. Powell
Author of "Life Fulfilled"

While Trying published my book on my own I ran into many road blocks.

I was so drained from all of the different tasks and avenues it took to get published.

I then was referred to Kelly through a friend.

Best decision I could have made. **Process was smooth and easy.**

I wrote the book and he made it available to the world.

Thanks man.

Mario Lattimore
Author of "Next Door"

You are SPECIAL!

Remember that! You are a unique individual. No one has lived your life like you have - and no one is more ready to advise, help or encourage other people who are facing or about to face what you have.

That's why it's only one question left to ask...

Are you ready to become a Best Selling Author?!

So I know you might be asking, "What's the catch?" Well, truthfully, there is a catch...

Only 50 (And Shrinking Fast) New Authors Will Be Accepted Into Our Publishing Program for this season!

We have placed a cap on the *Publishing* program at 50 new authors at a time. We want to be available for authors questions and to help them with marketing their new book. With our current work load, that's all we can handle. Once these slots have been filled (and this will not take long out of the thousands on our list) we will close the program.

If you want to Grow Your Business by becoming a Best Selling Author, the time to do it is right now before it's too late.

(**Warning:** This offer will be removed without warning and it will likely be months before access is available again.)

Get Started Now While Spots Are Still Available...

Sure, you could continue to do what you've done in the past and get the *same results*. Or...

... you could **TAKE ACTION NOW!**

Nothing is like being a real, Best Selling author. Imagine showing your friends or family members the Amazon.com site and YOUR book is on there!

They'll be staring at the site asking, "That's really *your* book?" (Yes, that's the first question they'll ask.)

And, you'll just smile and nod because you know — deep inside — that you've finally made it. You are a best selling author and your books are selling...

If you won't do this for yourself, think of your business and how your clients will view you after you hand them a signed copy.

What are you waiting for? You know this is what you need to do. Don't procrastinate. **Act now!**

Here is what you get with our
VIP PACKAGE:

- Physical Distribution Your Book to Amazon.com, Barnes & Noble.com, Books-A-Million.com!

- Digital Distribution to Amazon Kindle, iBooks, Barnes & Noble -Nook, Sony Reader Store, Kobo

- Complete Your Book Editing

- Complete Your Book Formatting

- Provide You With A Unique ISBN #

- Provide With A Professional Book Cover Design

- Provide You With An Electronic Proof Of Your Book

- Provide You With 1 Physical Proof Of Your Book

- Best Seller Marketing Plan

- Coach You on Implementing Our Amazon Best Seller Marketing Plan

- 200 Physical Copies of Your Book

- Create 2 Book Trailers / Promo Videos To Help Generate Sales

- Create A Social Media Banner To Help Promote Your Book

- Set-up Your Book For On-Demand Printing & Shipping

- A Press Release Written and Distributed Online

- Setup 2 Online Radio Interviews For You To Tell Your Story And Talk About Your Book.

- Promotion On All Of Our Social Media Outlets.

- Social Media Banners For All Your Platforms

- 2 Blog placements with articles or interviews about you and your book.

- 1,000 Full Color Front/Back (2x8) Bookmarks

- Full Color 31.5" x 78" Retractable Roll Up Standing Banner

- Plus You Will Maintain All Rights To Your Work & 100% Of Your Profits.

Plus you will receive a link to order your book wholesale for as low as $2.15 per book!

Get Started Now Visit:
www.PublishingAdvantageGroup.com
or Call 276-229-0530

(**Warning:** This offer will be removed without warning and it will likely be months before access is available again.)

Remember, you have absolutely nothing to lose!

Every second you don't have your book out you are missing out as people are constantly looking for that one person who has separated its self from the crowd.

I could go on and on with the possibilities. But I'm going to leave the rest to your imagination. I think you know It's Time!

Get Started Now Visit:
www.PublishingAdvantageGroup.com
or Call 276-229-0530

Will You Be The Next Best Selling Author Whose Work is Respected And Admired By The World?

Here Is Why You Should Get Signed Up Now!

- **You Gain Instant Respect And Admiration** – Best Selling Authors are perceived by the public like celebrities, who have achieved a goal that few people can. This automatically creates a feeling of respect and admiration in those who hear your name.

- **It Leads To Increased Business** – One of the key reasons anyone will do business with you is because of your credibility. The number one way to improve your credibility is to write a book. It Will Multiply Your Income – Aside from the revenue that you can generate through selling your books, you can also charge higher hourly fees for appearances, services or consultations simply because your level of credibility and knowledge is higher than those who are not published authors.

- **It Opens The Door To Opportunities** – People call upon the help of Best Selling Authors more than just about anyone else because they have proven that they not only have specialized knowledge on a specific topic, but they are capable of using that knowledge to help others.

- **It Separates You From The Rest** – In the expert industry where everyone is striving to be a guru, the best selling authors are the ones that most people view as true experts.

Now ask yourself this question; "How much is it worth to me to FINALLY get my book and my message into the hands of the world and increase my credibility and income exponentially at the same time?"

After all, this is not some "idea" that we think might work. This is a proven tool that will transform you from someone who plans on writing a book someday to a best selling author whose legacy will shine forever no time flat.

And quite honestly, that's not a tool that many people can claim to have created so it's no wonder why people are willing to pay top dollar for the best.

But here's the deal. We're not looking to make a fortune from this project. Instead, we're looking to help as many people as we possibly can.

And to do that, we know that we practically have to GIVE it away.

Get Started Now Visit:
www.PublishingAdvantageGroup.com
or Call 276-229-0530

Now we've done our part.

Now it's your turn.

It's your turn to take action and put your plans in motion.

So let's look again at everything you're getting, and what's in it for you.

- Physical Distribution Your Book to Amazon.com, Barnes & Noble.com, Books-A-Million.com!

- Digital Distribution to Amazon Kindle, iBooks, Barnes & Noble -Nook, Sony Reader Store, Kobo

- Complete Your Book Editing

- Complete Your Book Formatting

- Provide You With A Unique ISBN #

- Provide With A Professional Book Cover Design

- Provide You With An Electronic Proof Of Your Book

- Provide You With 1 Physical Proof Of Your Book

- Best Seller Marketing Plan

- Coach You on Implementing Our Amazon Best Seller Marketing Plan

- 200 Physical Copies of Your Book

- Create 2 Book Trailers / Promo Videos To Help Generate Sales

- Create A Social Media Banner To Help Promote Your Book

- Set-up Your Book For On-Demand Printing & Shipping

- A Press Release Written and Distributed Online

- Setup 2 Online Radio Interviews For You To Tell Your Story And Talk About Your Book.

- Promotion On All Of Our Social Media Outlets.

- Social Media Banners For All Your Platforms

- 2 Blog placements with articles or interviews about you and your book.

- 1,000 Full Color Front/Back (2x8) Bookmarks

- Full Color 31.5" x 78" Retractable Roll Up Standing Banner

- Plus You Will Maintain All Rights To Your Work & 100% Of Your Profits.

Plus you will receive a link to order your book wholesale for as low as $2.15 per book!

Remember, you have **nothing** to lose… except the rare opportunity to finally become a best selling author.

Get Started Now Visit:
www.PublishingAdvantageGroup.com
or Call 276-229-0530

www.ingramcontent.com/pod-product-compliance
Lightning Source LLC
Chambersburg PA
CBHW070728180526
45167CB00004B/1663